——— Stuff Every ———
COLLEGE
STUDENT
——— Should Know ———

Copyright © 2014 by Quirk Productions, Inc.
All rights reserved. No part of this book may be reproduced in any form
without written permission from the publisher.

Library of Congress Cataloging in Publication Number: 2013911678

ISBN: 978-1-59474710-6

Printed in China
Typeset in Goudy and Franklin Gothic

Designed by Amanda Richmond
Production management by John J. McGurk

Quirk Books
215 Church Street
Philadelphia, PA 19106
quirkbooks.com

10   9   8   7   6   5   4   3   2   1

—— Stuff Every ——
COLLEGE
STUDENT
—— Should Know ——

By Blair Thornburgh

QUIRK
BOOKS

To everyone on Team Burton-Judson

"If you're not having fun, you're doing it wrong."

Introduction

> "I do believe . . . all such citizens
> have two countries: one of their nature,
> and one of their citizenship."
> —Cicero, *De Legibus*, Book II, Section V

> "We can do anything we want!
> We're college students!"
> —*National Lampoon's Animal House* (1978)

You're about to learn a lot. Not just from this book—though, obviously, there's plenty of good stuff here—but from your whole college experience.

College is unlike any other time in your life. For many, college means independence, exploration, and finally living away from home; for others, college mainly means doing your own laundry for the first time. Either way, college is a time of change. You're leaving the people and places you've known for the past 18 years and going to a totally new place you chose yourself (or that chose you, as it were). Being a college student is like having dual citizenship: you belong to the home and community you were born into and to a new community driven and defined by people with intellectual pursuits like yours.

Oh, and you can do anything you want. You're a *college student*.

You're going to meet new people, you're going to go to class, you're going to *forget* to go to class, you're going to oversleep and pull all-nighters and survive on nothing but pizza and Lucky Charms, and, yes, you're going to learn from all of these things. You'll read books that will change the way you see things, shake up your status quo, and totally blow your mind. This is probably not one of those books. But with any luck, this little guide will help you through the sticky spots and be no less valuable to your education.

DORM LIVING
AND
PERSONAL
CARE

How to Make Your Dorm Room Livable . . . for No Money

For the next few semesters, your dorm room is your castle . . . but cinder blocks and linoleum don't exactly scream *homey*. Here's how to make your new home cozier.

• **Beg and borrow.** Ask family and friends if they've got any old furniture, lighting, or decorations they're dying to get rid of. When you get your room assignment, reach out to your new roommate so the two of you can discuss who can scrounge what (you only need one mini fridge). If you can stand to strip down your home bedroom, it's easy enough to bring along some familiar stuff. But remember that your new space might not have room for that full-size loveseat or a ceiling that can handle your light-up disco ball.

- **Find free (or cheap) stuff.** Beat the move-in-day rush and scope out sites like Craigslist or FreeCycle before you even get to town. Search the campus online classifieds early and often. The closer it gets to a time of major exodus (like the end of a semester), the likelier you are to find an everything-must-go buyer's market of furniture and appliances.

- **Be ready to clean house.** Don't count on your dorm room having been cleaned recently (or ever). Bring along essentials like a broom, a dustpan, sprayable surface cleaner, disinfecting wipes, and a few sponges (you can send the cleaning supplies home with your parents if it turns out your dorm keeps some on hand). A quick sweep and surface wipe-down on move-in day will (literally) brighten your space.

- **Hang some curtains.** The standard-issue roll-down shade is depressing. Even the cheapest pair of drapes will make your dorm look more like a bedroom and less like a cellblock.

- **Throw down a rug.** A colorful floor covering makes a room cozy and comfortable. Keep it low-pile (no shag!) unless you have access to a vacuum; thicker rugs will get grody.

- **Invest in mood lighting.** Harsh overhead fluorescents are for supermarkets, not your home away from home. A good floor lamp, desk light, and even some strings of Christmas lights are warmer and easier on the eyes. Or replace the existing bulbs with "natural light" versions that shine the full spectrum of light waves, which keep study-related eyestrain at bay.

- **Get comfortable.** Ample pillows and blankets are obviously a must, but a mattress pad or foam "egg crate" (or both) can transform a dorm bed from rock hard to super comfy.

- **Set up a message board.** In the dark ages before the Internet, *wall post* meant a handwritten message stuck on a physical wall. And the concept still works! Hang a chalkboard or dry-erase board on your door for notes/doodles/hieroglyphics from visitors.

How to Cook with a Microwave

What to do when you want a hot meal but the dining hall's closed and takeout is too much trouble (or too expensive)? Turn to dorm room cookery. Your microwave oven can do so much more than reanimate lackluster leftovers.

- **Scramble eggs** by greasing a microwave-safe bowl and beating together two eggs with a fork. Nuke on high power for 1 minute and then continue cooking in 30-second intervals until eggs are done to your liking.

- **Steam vegetables** with a microwave steamer, or steamable plastic bags (find them in the grocery store), or in a covered microwave-safe bowl with 2–3 tablespoons water.

- **Microwave popcorn** (not the fake-butter kind that causes cancer in lab rats) is easy to make: Add around ¼ cup unpopped kernels to a plain brown-paper lunch bag, and fold down the end of the bag a few times to close. Microwave on high for 2–3 minutes, or until there's about 5 seconds between pops (after you've done it a few times, you'll figure out the best timing for your microwave). Season to taste with salt, oil or butter, Parmesan, powdered garlic, or chili powder (or all of the above).

- **Make real easy mac and cheese:** Combine ⅓ cup pasta with ½ cup water in a mug and microwave on high power for 2 minutes. Stir (be careful not to burn yourself!). Cook for 2–4 more 2-minute intervals, stirring after each, and then stir in ¼ cup milk and ½ cup shredded cheddar cheese.

- **Bake a personal-sized chocolate-chip cookie:** Melt 1 tablespoon butter in a mug on 70 percent power. Add 3 drops vanilla extract, pinch salt, 1 tablespoon each brown and white sugar, 1 egg yolk, scant ¼ cup flour, and 2 tablespoons chocolate chips, stirring after each addition. Microwave on 70 percent power for 40 seconds—if it isn't done, blast it with another 10-second interval or two.

How to Cook without a Microwave

Don't have a microwave in your room? Don't fret. Here are some other options.

- **Just add water.** An electric kettle can be as central to the college experience as all-nighters and toga parties. Liven up standard ramen noodles and instant oatmeal with stirred-in sauces and spices, and look for novel cut-and-dried options like instant miso soup, couscous, and curries. Keep a few tea bags on hand for a caffeine dose that's more nudge than kick (or opt for herbal infusions).

- **Heat it with an iron.** Obviously, the first ingredient here is a *huge pinch of caution*. Never leave an iron unattended. Irons are designed to make clothes— not food—hot and flat. That said, if you know what you're doing, your iron can make a mean melty sandwich. Here's how:

1. Set iron to cotton or linen setting and make sure steam is off. Cover a (heatproof) surface with two heavy-duty aluminum foil sheets.

2. Top a bread slice (or tortilla) with meltable fillings: cheese and salsa, peanut butter and banana slices, whatever your hungry heart desires. Cover with another bread slice and two more foil sheets, and fold over edges to avoid oozage.

3. Press iron onto the foil packet and move it back and forth across the foil surface for 30 seconds. Carefully flip the packet and repeat on the other side. Carefully unfold the foil a bit to assess the level of melt. Repeat if necessary.

- **Cook in a kiddie oven.** Don't be in a hurry to put the kid stuff away: the lightbulb-powered plastic cookie bakers of your youth (think Easy-Bake) make perfect dorm-room snack machines. Pick one up at a yard sale and order baking mixes online, then plug that sucker in and become the most popular person on your floor.

How to Brew Better Coffee

If caffeine's all you care about, instant coffee is your friend. But if you want a cup that doesn't taste like rehydrated dirt particles, try one of these low-tech, high-flavor options. For the freshest possible cup, buy whole beans and use a hand-powered grinder (available online or at specialty coffee stores).

- **Pour-over brewers** are funnel-shaped ceramic or plastic devices that look like teacups with holes in the bottom. Place brewer onto a cup and put a paper coffee filter in the funnel. Add 2 tablespoons ground coffee for every 8 ounces water (you may need more than 8 ounces if your cup is big), and then add enough boiling water to saturate the grounds. Continue steadily pouring water into the brewer so that it remains about one-half to three-quarters full while the coffee drips into the cup below.

- **A French press** is a glass container with a fitted plunger lid. Add 2 level tablespoons ground coffee for every 8 ounces water, top with boiling water, stir with a wooden spoon or chopstick (metal can crack the glass), and brew for 4 minutes. Then press the plunger down and pour into cups.

- **For iced coffee,** start the night before. Combine ½ cup ground coffee with 8 cups water in a French press or other container, such as a glass jar. Stir, let steep overnight, and strain in the morning; if using a jar, strain through paper coffee filters. Store in the fridge for up to 2 weeks. To serve, dilute to taste with water or milk.

How to Keep Your Mini Fridge Clean

Even if you believe that *every* pizza is a personal pizza, leftovers are inevitable—but letting your mini fridge turn into a petri dish isn't. Follow these precautions to keep germs at bay.

- **'Frigerate promptly.** Food-borne bacteria loves lukewarm grub, so the sooner you pop those leftovers into the fridge, the less time the creepy crawlies have to be fruitful and multiply. If food has been left at room temperature for more than four hours after preparation, chuck it.

- **Store your food in airtight conditions.** Invest in a set of snap-lid plastic containers, zip-top bags, and aluminum foil to keep your goodies from drying out and getting crusty.

- **Heed the sell-by and best-before dates on the labels,** especially for dairy and meat products. If you can't tell if something is milk or cottage cheese, toss it.

- **When in doubt, throw it out.** Rhyming advice is never wrong! Even if last week's burrito hasn't sprouted a visible penicillin culture, it's probably overstayed its welcome; some bacteria and molds are stealthy.

- **Don't crowd.** The more stuff in your fridge, the less cold air can get around all your stuff. Leave some breathing room to keep everything chilly.

- **Wipe it out.** If the fridge (or its shelves) starts to get funky, make a cleaning solution with 1–2 tablespoons of baking soda and about a quart of warm water and wipe down all surfaces.

WHEN TO THROW OUT LEFTOVERS
(ASSUMING THEY'VE BEEN STORED PROPERLY)

FOOD	THROW OUT AFTER
Chicken fingers or nuggets	1–2 days
Pizza	3–5 days
Soft cheese (like string cheese)	2 weeks
Hard cheese (like cheddar or Gouda)	2–3 weeks
Frozen food	3–4 months (in freezer)
Egg, chicken, or tuna salad	3–5 days
Takeout (Chinese, Indian, etc.) with meat	3–4 days
Lunch meats, opened	3–5 days
Hard-boiled eggs	1 week
Milk or yogurt	1 week
Rice	1–2 days

How to Avoid the Freshman 15

First of all, *relax*: studies have shown that first-year weight gain is usually more like the Freshman 3 to 5. And, these days, more and more campuses have health-friendly amenities like high-tech gyms and endlessly verdant salad bars. All you've got to do is eat well, drink water, and be merry.

- **Dine smart.** Forget the sundae stations, pasta bars, and deep-fried delicacies. Fill half your plate at the salad bar, and then divide the rest of the space between protein (eggs, lean meats, beans, fish, or tofu) and whole grains or fruit. When in doubt, look for food in as close to its natural state as possible (a baked potato is better than a tater tot), and remember: all-you-can-eat is a suggestion, not a *challenge*.

- **Snack wisely.** Shoot for foods that are high in protein, fiber, or both, like yogurt, peanut butter and whole-grain crackers, veggies and hummus, or fruit. If your dining plan lets you take snacks on the go, swipe something healthy every time you visit and keep a stockpile in your dorm room for hunger emergencies.

- **Don't drink extra calories.** It's not just sodas and grande Frappuccinos that add to your caloric bottom line—fruit juices and energy drinks can both hide loads of sugar.

- **Get a grip on social grazing.** It's easy to inhale handfuls of Doritos when you're hanging out with friends. And while there's nothing wrong with a little late-night pizza—it is college, after all—think a slice or two, not half the pie. Snack slowly, and ask yourself if you're hungry or just eating out of boredom.

- **Work out.** These days, it's hard to find a college whose tuition doesn't cover a free or cheap gym membership. Whether it's swimming laps, lifting weights, or logging time on the treadmill a couple times a week, take advantage of this benefit and burn some calories.

- **Join a team.** Most colleges have club, intramural, or noncompetitive sports that are open to everyone—nonjocks included. The name of the game is fun, even if the sport is technically called ultimate frisbee or kickball.

- **Ditch your car.** If you live off campus but nearby, try walking or biking to class instead of tooling around on four wheels. All those steps add up—and you'll save on gas money. If you must drive, park in a more distant lot to build some walking time into your day.

- **Stay hydrated.** This means water, not coffee, soda, or alcohol. Drinking H_2O only will save you calories and help you feel full for longer. Keep a bottle in your bag for class, and if you must indulge in something fizzy at the dining hall, stick to seltzer.

HEALTHY DINING HALL SWAPS

INSTEAD OF	TRY
French fries	Baked sweet potato (less fat, more vitamin A and fiber)
Iceberg lettuce	Baby spinach (more iron and vitamin A)
Flavored yogurt	Cottage cheese or plain Greek yogurt with fruit (more protein, less sugar)
Cereal or anything with mini marshmallows	Whole-grain cereal or or oatmeal with fruit (more fiber, less sugar)
Hamburger	Turkey burger (less fat)
Soda	Seltzer with lemon wedge (less sugar and caffeine)
Prepared salad dressing	A sprinkle of olive oil and vinegar (less sugar and fat)
Mac and cheese	Vegetable stir-fry with tofu (more protein, more vegetables, still meatless)
Fruit cups or fruit in syrup	Whole fruits (less sugar, more portability!)

How to Take Care of Yourself When You're Sick

Being independent from your parents is awesome . . . until you get the flu and realize there's no one to bring you chicken soup. Sure, it's a bummer, but it doesn't mean you're going to die (even if you feel like you might). Unfortunately, campuses are breeding grounds for illness, so be prepared to face down a nasty bug or two during your college career. Here's how to nurse and doctor yourself back to health.

- **Get your shots.** Before you even set foot on your new campus, make sure your family doctor has you properly immunized: serious, life-threatening diseases that can run rampant through dorms (like meningitis) are preventable with a one-time jab. Once school's in session, many campuses will offer free or cheap flu shots, too—even if you hate needles, you'll probably hate a week of fevers even more.

- **Miss class.** If you're feeling bad, stay home. No one wants your disease-vectory self coughing all over the handouts and infecting the rest of your discussion group. Shoot a short, honest e-mail to your professor or TA to stay on top of class work (see page 45).

- **Rest.** Ask (or bribe) your roommate to clear out so you can convalesce in peace (although, depending on how sick you are, you might not even have to ask). Once you've got the place to yourself, make sure you actually sleep— playing video games or zoning out in front of Netflix doesn't count.

- **Call in favors.** Just because you're in the Real World doesn't mean you have to fend completely for yourself. If you're too sick to leave bed, ask a friend to pick up soup, cough drops, and ginger ale (for you) and hand sanitizer (for your friend). And pay your helpers in kind when they're the ones in self-imposed quarantine.

- **Be your own doctor, but only to a point.** For mild to moderate illness, there are plenty of easy home cures (see below). If the situation is more serious, though, don't DIY. If you've got a high fever or an unshakable cough or can't keep down food and liquids, get to your campus health center ASAP.

SYMPTOM	HOME TREATMENT
Mild fever	Over-the-counter pain reliever/fever reducer containing acetaminophen, ibuprofen, or naproxen; cold compress
Sore throat	Hot tea with lemon and honey; gargle with salt water
Upset stomach	Seltzer; mint or ginger tea; simple, starchy foods (bananas, toast, rice)
Head congestion	Saline solution and neti pot (find one at drugstores or online); spicy food
Chest cold	Over-the-counter medicines with guaifenesin; mentholated ointment (like Vicks); steamy showers; mist humidifier

How to Do Laundry

There's no avoiding it: clothes must be washed, and preferably *before* every shirt becomes a de facto sweatshirt. Here are some down and dirty tips to get your duds clean.

- **Sort by color.** Put darks in one load, lights in the other. Cold water will work fine for both (and saves energy, too). If you must use hot water, save it for your lights (and be extra sure there are no dark stowaways, to avoid the dread pink-shirt effect).

- **Cache some coins.** If your dorm uses coin-op machines, keep a change jar in your room to stock up on precious quarters (make sure to bring enough for the dryer, too!).

- **Read the tags.** Pay attention to the care tags on the inside of clothes (see chart on page 35) and follow the directions. Wash stretchy items like bras and tights in a mesh laundry bag so they don't get snared on washing machine innards. When in doubt, hand-wash: most laundry rooms have a sink you can use to swish your delicates around in. Rinse thoroughly (twice!), roll in a towel, and then lay flat to dry.

- **Use detergent wisely.** A full cap is usually too much: the inside of the cap should be marked with a (nearly invisible) line indicating the proper amount for a single load. Buy concentrated detergent so you don't have to lug around giant jugs of soap.

- **Dry, dry, dry.** Double-check garment labels for drying info, and then load your dryer-friendly pieces into the machine. Clean the lint trap before you fire up the dryer—look for a removable screen somewhere near the door. High heat is generally okay for most clothes, but follow the label instructions. Air-dry delicates on a drying rack, hangers, or even the foot of your bed.

- **Keep a watchful eye.** Set a timer on your phone and don't wander too far—you don't want to be the person whose gobs of wet clothes are tying up the machines.

GUIDE TO LAUNDRY TAG SYMBOLS

WASHING

 1. 2. 3. 4. 5.

1. machine wash cold 2. machine wash warm
3. machine wash hot 4. hand wash 5. do not wash

DRYING

1. tumble dry no heat 2. tumble dry low heat 3. tumble dry
medium heat, 4. tumble dry high heat, 5. do not tumble dry
6. line dry 7. drip dry 8. dry flat

IRONING

 1. 2. 3. 4. 5.

1. iron steam or dry with low heat 2. iron steam or dry with
medium heat 3. iron steam or dry with high heat
4. do not iron with steam 5. do not iron

BLEACHING

 1. 2. 3.

1. bleach as needed 2. nonchlorine bleach as needed
3. do not bleach

DRY-CLEANING

1. ◯ 2.

1. dry-clean 2. do not dry-clean

How to Be a Good Roommate

College is a lot like preschool . . . at least when it comes to getting along. The same basic rules you learned over finger paints and nap time come back into play when you're paired up to live with a total stranger. Here are the highlights:

- **Be friendly.** You don't have to become your roomie's best friend, but it never hurts to smile and have a casual chat now and then. Extra points for helping roommates keep a level head during exam season or fetching medicine when they're sick.

- **Share.** Yes, you're kind of required to if you're living in the same room, but a little generosity goes a long way. Invest in some agreed-upon communal amenities (anything from snacks to speakers) and be gracious if your roomie wants to steal a shirt for a party (even if you say no).

- **Lay down some ground rules.** It's a good idea to establish a baseline for tricky situations *before* there's a problem. Don't just assume that you'll figure it out; speak up. Anything from early alarm clocks to who's buying toilet paper to—ahem—late-night personal visitors can be problematic if left unaddressed.

- **Use your words.** If something is bugging you, let your roommate know (nicely!) and try to hash it out. Suggestions, not accusations, are the way to go, and make sure *you're* open to listening, too. If you two run into a real problem, don't be afraid to enlist help from the residence staff (RAs, dorm managers, or faculty dorm sponsors).

- **Give your roomie some space.** Even if you do end up being buddies with the person sharing your sleeping space, everyone needs privacy from time to time. Clear out when you can, and let your cohabitant have free rein of the room once in a while.

- **Don't be that guy (or girl).** When your roommate's around, err on the side of good behavior. Respecting someone's privacy also means observing your own, so save all your potentially gross personal behavior for alone time. If you do end up, say, puking on the floor or letting old takeout turn into a crusty science experiment, just apologize, clean up, and do your best not to do it again.

WHAT TO SAY WHEN YOUR ROOMMATE . . .

. . . won't keep the room clean.

"I know you've been busy with classes, but could you be sure to take the garbage out today? I don't want us to get bugs."

. . . steals your stuff.

"Can you let me know if you want to borrow my shirt? I'm sure you just forgot to ask, but I was going to wear it out tonight."

. . . keeps you up talking at night.

"Would you mind hanging out in a different room if you're going to be up past midnight? I have an early class."

. . . constantly blasts music.

"Could you wear headphones when I'm around? I want to listen to my own stuff."

. . . gets it on a little too often.

"I totally respect your right to privacy, but I feel like I'm getting locked out of my own room. Can we work out a sharing system?"

. . . wants to be your new BFF.

"I'm sorry, my schedule is so crazy right now. How about we hit the dining hall together on Sundays?"

. . . won't give you privacy.

"I'd ask you to stay while I get dressed, but I really only like you as a friend."

ACADEMIC
LIFE

How to
Take Notes

Apart from showing up to class, notetaking is probably the most important trick of the academic trade. But just because it's a basic skill doesn't mean it's intuitive. So take note of these tips:

- **Know why you're taking notes.** Notes have two purposes: they help you listen better in class, and they help you study better after class. Writing things down as you hear them actually helps you hear them better, and having the key points on paper makes it possible (or at least way easier) to review them come study time.

- **Pick a medium.** If your thoughts come faster via keyboard (and your professor allows laptops), go ahead and type. If not, equip yourself with a decent notebook with whatever guidelines are most helpful: graph paper, college ruling, or blank pages.

- **Don't take minutes.** You're a student, not a stenographer. You don't need every last detail of the lecture or discussion; in fact, focusing on getting all the minutiae often blinds you to the bigger picture.

- **If it's on the board, it goes on your page.** If you take only one note-taking technique to heart, make it this one. Anything essential enough for your professor or TA to put on the board must go into your notes (especially stuff that's underlined, circled, or repeatedly tapped/laser-pointered-at).

- **Piggyback on PowerPoint.** If your professor makes lecture slide shows available before class, print them (leave space for notes) and bring them to class to scribble on. On the other hand, if you can't get an advance copy, don't blindly copy every single thing on the slides into your notes during the lecture. It's much easier for your instructor to throw something into a PowerPoint than to write it on the board; just because it's included doesn't guarantee that it's relevant.

- **Focus on the facts.** Names, dates, equations, definitions, theories, postulates, titles, and other hard facts should all be noted.

- **Go abstract.** If the topic at hand isn't cut-and-dried and list friendly—maybe it's a debate or a series of relationships—try mapping information with circles, flowcharts, or another visual form that makes sense (this is where that unlined paper comes in handy).

- **Try the Cornell system.** Draw a vertical line down the page about two inches in from the left edge, diving the page into a larger and a smaller column. During class, write all your notes in the larger column, and when class is over, sum up the most important concepts in the smaller column. This system sets you up for studying: cover either column and try to remember as much information as you can based on the cues you can see.

How to E-mail a Professor

Gone are the days when pneumatic tubes and confusing cubbyhole message systems were your sole options for extracurricular communication. Whether you're begging for a paper extension, asking to meet for office hours, or submitting a paper, an e-mail to your professor is now the normal mode of contact. Follow this advice to make sure you get your message across clearly.

- **Don't wait.** Sooner is better, especially if you're going to miss class or asking for a flexible deadline.

- **Avoid vauge subject lines.** "Question" is not a great subject line; "question about Tuesday's reading assignment" is.

- **Say hello . . . properly.** Get your prof's title correct, and avoid casual-sounding salutations like "hey" or "hi." "Dear Professor X" is a universally acceptable default (but unless you're Wolverine, replace X with the prof's actual surname).

- **Introduce yourself.** Take pity on your professors—they teach many classes with many students. State your name, major, graduation year (if needed), and the course you're taking. Even if you're in an intimate seminar or discussion group, do the professor a favor and ID yourself preemptively.

- **Get to the point.** Write short, concise sentences that express what you want or need (see examples on pages 47–48). Be polite and resist the urge to be casual, but don't feel like you've got to write scintillating prose—an e-mail is still an e-mail.

- **Be specific.** Throw in as many pertinent facts and figures as you can: problem numbers, meeting times, TA names, page ranges, etc., will all help your instructor process your request faster.

- **Don't be cute.** Emoticons, shorthand, all caps, and long-winded signatures full of your favorite quotes are obnoxious. And proofread, *please*.

- **Say thanks and sign off.** "Sincerely" is a good all-purpose valediction; use your first and last name after.

- **Know the rules of attachment.** If you're submitting work via e-mail, double-check that you've got your document formatted the way your professor asked for it. When in doubt, ask a TA.

- **Be patient and acknowledge receipt.** Professors are busy people. Don't expect an immediate reply. If your professor responds with the handout or info you needed, send a quick "thank you!" e-mail to confirm that you received it.

Sample E-mails

Dear Professor Jones,
My name is Grace Fisher and I'm a sophomore student in ENGL1020, section 02. I'm writing to ask about the assignment for Thursday: the syllabus lists a reading assignment but no written response, and I wanted to make sure nothing is due to hand in. Thank you for your help.
Sincerely,
Grace Fisher

Dear Professor Sentman,
My name is Rachel Schorr and I'm a third-year undergraduate student in PHYS3400, lab section B. Unfortunately, I've come down with the flu that's going around and I'm too ill to attend the lab this afternoon. Please let me know how I can make up the lab work, and I'll be sure to do so as soon as I'm feeling better. Thank you.
Sincerely,
Rachel Schorr

Dear Professor White,
My name is Samuel Li, and I'm a student in the Introduction to Renaissance Art seminar. I am writing in regards to the midterm paper due Friday. I was traveling last week with the Debate Team and did not have as much free time as I'd anticipated to get my research in shape. I'd appreciate it very much if you would grant me a small extension until Monday morning. My outline is ready to go, but it would be very helpful not to have to rush to finish the writing. Please let me know if this is possible, and thank you very much.
Sincerely,
Samuel Li

How to Form a (Useful) Study Group

When it comes to tackling complex topics, a study group can either go the "many hands make light work" route or quickly deteriorate to "none of us is as dumb as all of us." If your class material could benefit from some good groupthink, follow these tips for a productive meeting of the minds.

- **Keep the group on the small side.** Three or four people is best. Five is doable, but more than that and you might as well just invite your whole section. The ideal group members aren't your best friends (since you're not likely to want to work together), but they're not the annoying know-it-alls you get into heated debates with in class, either. Pick people whom you can tolerate and who seem likely not to flake.

- **Decide how you'll communicate.** E-mail and texts are fine for hashing out meeting times, but it's also a good idea to create some kind of digital home base (like a shared Dropbox folder, Google doc, or class-related message board) where your group can store problem sets, review sheets, and the like.

- **Make a schedule.** A study group is only good if it actually groups up. Specify not just when you'll get together, but where and for how long (no one wants to rove around the library looking for a table all night). Give yourself enough time, but not *too* much: two hours is optimum. See if you can reserve a dedicated group-study space at the library or take over an empty classroom.

- **Decide what you'll cover.** Tag-teaming vocabulary or problem sets is fine, but also save some time to go over *concepts* covered in the lectures since your last study session; you might actually learn something together.

- **Follow the rules.** Make sure that your instructor is cool with collaboration on projects and assignments. Don't use your group to steal other people's work. And remember you can't take the test as a group.

- **Try taking turns.** Assign each person a cert-ain topic or specific lecture, and then have them "teach" it back to the rest of you (which actually helps the teacher as much as the teach-ees).

- **Don't freak out if an argument springs up.** Turn your group's warring philosophies on the topic into a productive debate on the subject material.

- **Prioritize.** Unless you're up for marathon-length study sessions, you probably won't cover every part of the homework or lecture material. Have everyone come armed with questions, and wrap things up with a clear sense of what you'll review individually before the next meeting.

How to Study

Unless you like to live on the edge of academic probation, studying is as nonnegotiable as note-taking. Fortunately, you've been taking great notes, so all you've got to do now is just focus, buckle down, and . . . study. Which means what, exactly? This:

- **Plan out a reasonable study schedule,** for both semester-long study and pre-exam prep. Unlike in high school, you'll probably get a reading period (anywhere from a few days to a week or two) before finals—so block out that time and use it wisely.

- **Find a distraction-free study zone.** Ideally, it should be a place where you do nothing but study, so your brain knows to flip into focus mode as soon as you cross the threshold. If the library's too creepy-quiet for you, try a coffee shop (bonus: caffeine!), your dorm's common room, or a quiet corner of the dining hall.

- **Break it up.** If you're having trouble getting started, set a timer for 20 minutes of study, followed by a five-minute break—smaller chunks of time are less daunting and more effective for helping you retain what you learn.

- **Flash some cards.** For courses with extensive memorization (math, science, language vocabulary), flash cards are an excellent tool—but only if you use them effectively. Resist the urge to toss a card in the *Done* pile after one right answer; keep it in circulation for a few more rounds. Then flip the cards to the second side and go through them backwards.

- **Create review sheets** using your class notes to reload all that important information into your brain. Instead of relying on review sheets created by your instructor or other students, go through your own notes chronologically and re-write them carefully. A neat 'n' tidy list of facts isn't nearly as helpful as the act of making it.

- **Make lists.** Once you've created a review sheet, compile some homemade cross-indexes: pull out the categories, themes, or overarching ideas of the course material, and list other, smaller concepts underneath them. If you're not the ruled-paper type, try connecting related concepts in circles.

- **Use whatever materials your instructor provides.** If you're permitted outlines for in-class essays or equation sheets for exams, bring them. If the instructor or TA provides practice problems, do them. If your professor bolds, underlines, *and* italicizes something on the syllabus, ***it is definitely important.***

- **Don't sprint.** Think of the process like a marathon and don't expect to get everything down pat in a single study session. If you feel your focus flagging, take a break or switch to a different subject. Cramming and all-nighters are not good ways to study. Still, things happen. So, if you must . . .

How to Pull an All-Nighter

It's 9:30 p.m. You need to write 30 pages of your final paper, and the deadline is just 10 ½ hours away. Don't panic: like all cultural rites of passage, pulling an all-nighter is as character building as it is vastly overhyped. The paper will get written, and you're not going to die (not from this, anyway). Just follow this syllabus:

- **Prep your environment.** Grab any and all necessary study materials (don't forget power cords and earbuds) and find somewhere secluded where you can concentrate. If you can, flip on all the lights and turn down the thermostat (or open a window): bright light and cool temperatures keep you uncomfortably alert (i.e., awake).

- **Use technology wisely.** If your computer is more likely to take you to Facebook than to Google Scholar, install a distraction-blocking extension for your Internet browser to block time-wasting websites, or consider ditching your laptop altogether if you can study without it. Load up your smartphone with useful apps: relaxing music or white noise, a timer (to help you work in chunks), an alarm (set one—or two—even if you think you won't nod off), and a caffeine-optimization app (seriously) to maximize your buzz (see below).

- **Fuel properly.** Eat a light dinner and pop a piece of peppermint gum; the cool, peppery flavor is a natural stimulant. Stay hydrated during the night by drinking at least 8 ounces of water per hour; you'll stave off headaches and have an excuse for some periodic leg-stretching en route to the bathroom.

- **Caffeinate.** Unless you have synapses of steel, caffeine is nonnegotiable. Usually, the sweet spot is 300 milligrams, so pick your poison and dose accordingly.

- **Plan your attack.** Take a few minutes to get organized before getting started and you'll avoid floundering later. Don't dive right into writing a paper if you have no idea what to cover; make an outline, however scribbly, to organize your thoughts. For exam cramming, try creating an express version of a review sheet or flash cards.

- **Work in chunks.** If you have to write 30 pages in five hours, do your best to crank out six pages every hour (or one page every ten minutes, if you want to obsess). Don't spend too long on any single task; a finished, imperfect paper is better than nothing.

- **Get out of your seat periodically.** This will keep your blood flowing and stop you from falling asleep. Stretch your limbs, do a few jumping jacks, or stand on your head (advanced method) for a little physical pick-me-up.

- **Bribe yourself.** Sweeten the deal with whatever it takes—a cup of coffee for every three pages written, an M&M for every flash card memorized, or a disciplined break for Internet cat videos at the end of every chapter.

- **Sleep. But not a lot.** As little as 20 minutes of power-napping right before your test can help your poor fried brain function better. Set aside your last hour to wrap up, curl up, and wake up—you'll need at least fifteen minutes after opening your eyes to clear out the mental cobwebs. (Don't forget to give yourself time to get to class!) Above all, *set an alarm* or two, or give your roommate five bucks to forcibly shake you into consciousness. You've worked too hard to lose your progress to the snooze button.

CAFFEINE CHART

DRINK	AVERAGE CAFFEINE CONTENT, PER 8 OZ.
Brewed coffee	165 mg
Single-cup pod	112 mg
Instant coffee	99 mg
Espresso (single shot)	40 mg
Green tea	30 mg
Black tea	38 mg
Energy drink	75 mg
Cola	35 mg
Energy shot (2 oz.)	207 mg

How to Pass a Test You Forgot to Study For

You know that nightmare in which you're handed a test full of unfamiliar questions, and everyone around you is busily writing like they totally get it, and you're suddenly and inexplicably naked? This is like that, but with your clothes on. Whatever forces of fate conspire against you, sometimes you just have to go into that classroom cold, grab the test, and wing it. But with a few savvy strategies, you can salvage a passing grade.

General Strategies

- **Show up.** If you don't have time to study, try at least to come in rested, well fed, and optimally caffeinated. And don't be late.

- **Take it slow.** Misunderstanding a question is a tragic and frustrating way to lose points, but it's avoidable. Read through every question at least twice.

- **Check your work.** If you finish early, resist the urge to turn in your test immediately. Getting a question wrong even though you knew the answer will just make you feel worse.

- **Consider why you weren't prepared.** Do you need to set up pretest e-mail reminders for yourself? Hang an exam schedule next to your bed? Impose an Xbox moratorium during test weeks?

If It's an Essay Test

- **Write *something*.** Leaving a question blank guarantees you a zero, so even guessing wildly improves your odds of racking up some credit.

- **Write what you know.** Look for a way to connect the question to a subject familiar to you and craft your argument around that.

- **Make a statement.** A clear thesis and conclusion will give you the backbone of an argument, even if you can't flesh it out. Your first and last sentences should be clear and to the point—then you can spin your wheels and fill the in-between.

- **Speak the lingo.** Try to cram in as many concepts from class as you can: themes, ideas, catch phrases, whatever. Busy TAs sometimes grade essays with literal checklists for keywords, so don't hold back on jargon and specialized vocabulary. Or play the linguistic wunderkind and sprinkle in whatever bons mots you know (or can make up), à la this bullet point, and sound instantly brilliant. QED.

- **Start with the facts.** Figure out what facts you do know, and use those to describe a simple, logical pattern: cause and effect, if/then relationships, point and counterpoint, etc. Don't fall into circular reasoning ("The author's writing is ineffective because it doesn't do anything") or go off on tangents.

- **Play favorites.** If you know your professor has a pet idea, subject, or school of thought, write your essay like a brochure for the cause. Yes, this is borderline brownnosing, and it's not exactly educational, but we're talking about survival, not critical thinking.

If It's a Multiple Choice Test

- **Cross out** all the options you know are wrong right away—usually, two out of four answers will be clearly incorrect.

- **Zero in** on answers that repeat specific terms from the question, and look for key qualifying words like *always, never, all, none, the most, the least, usually,* etc., to refine your thinking.

- **Play the odds.** Answers with specific determiners, strange or unknown words, insults, jokes, or extreme choices tend to be incorrect. Answers with qualifiers, longer and more complete statements, or "all/none of the above" tend to be correct.

- **Run the numbers.** If two answers are opposites, one of them is likely to be the right choice. If the answers span a range of numbers (dates, years, statistics, percentages), the choice that falls in the middle tends to be correct.

- **Trust your gut.** If you have an instinct to go with an answer, don't second-guess. You may be tapping into a vague memory of a lecture or reading—and instinct is better than nothing.

- **Keep an eye on the patterns.** A test isn't likely to have a string of As or Bs, but it may go ADBCADBC or BACCABBACCAB.

- **Work quickly.** Be sure to finish. No single wrong answer is worth enough to sink your grade, but a couple of lucky guesses could save you from the brink of failure.

- **Come back to it later.** Don't waste too much time on any one question; get down as many as you can before puzzling out the trickier ones.

- **Stay in line.** If you're bubbling in circles on an answer sheet, or otherwise marking your answers separately from the test questions, make double-extra-sure that your responses line up properly to avoid a cascade of *incorrects*.

How to Pick a Major

Your major is, well, major: it will dictate everything from which classes you take to what gets calligraphed on your diploma to which jobs you eventually pursue. But don't let that freak you out: many schools don't require you to declare one until at least the end of your first year. And most students switch majors at least once. Do this before making your decision:

- **Try it out.** Before committing to any major, take a class (or two) in the subject and make sure you actually, you know, *enjoy studying it*. If during your first semester you're bogged down by required courses, see if you can sit in on a session or two.

- **Explore.** There's way more to college than the reading, 'riting, and 'rithmatic you had in high school, from the broad and theoretical (like International Studies, Comparative Literature, or Philosophy) to the niche (like Ancient Mesopotamian Languages). Pick up (or download) a copy of your school's course catalog and read it thoroughly to get a sense of the possibilities.

- **Think long-term.** If you know—or even think—you want to pursue graduate education (especially in a field like medicine or law), do your research as soon as possible. Some schools offer specific preprofessional majors and others don't, but most postgrad programs will require at least a few undergrad courses. Make sure that you'll have the right roster of classes to qualify.

- **Follow your heart.** Don't feel obligated or pressured to major in something because of what your parents tell you. While breaking from their wishes may not be easy—after all, you've spent 18 years more or less obeying them—remember that this is *your* future at stake. Passion is a great convincer, so make the case for your major, and if you still don't see eye to eye with your folks, agree to disagree.

- **Ignore the bottom line.** If your heart isn't in Economics, it doesn't matter how big a paycheck you'll bring in once you've taken over the private sector. Every major has the potential to be fulfilling; none is "useless" (if it were, why would the school even bother offering it?). Do what you love, not what's likely to make big bucks (of course, if you can swing both, by all means do so).

- **Reach for the stars.** Or shoot for the moon, or just generally aim high at astral bodies. Don't be put off by a field of study that's competitive or considered "tough," if it's what you want to pursue. Hard work and passion are the only ingredients you need for success (and a good class rank).

- **Bring your advisor on board.** Try to schedule a meeting with your academic advisor sometime in your first semester on campus. (Even if one is required, go again; there's no such thing as too much help.) Your advisor will take the agony out of plotting out your future course schedules, help you switch gears if you decide to change majors, and sometimes even pull strings to get you into that required class that's already overbooked (so be nice!).

How to Request a Faculty Recommendation

Whether you're going after a grad school spot, some work abroad, a fellowship, a volunteer program, or just an internship you don't hate, it's competitive out there. A letter of recommendation from one of your professors is rock-solid proof of character that will help you rise to the top of the applicant pile. Here's how to get one:

- **Establish a connection.** Before you even entertain the faintest notion of asking, make sure you stand out. You don't need to have solid As; in fact, a personal connection and participation in class is more likely to earn your professor's respect than a spotless academic record. Speak up during discussions, go to the professor's office hours, engage with the material outside of class however you can. When your name pops up, your professor should be able to picture your face.

- **Go with someone you know.** A well-written personal letter is better than a famous signature and paragraphs of generic praise from a rock-star professor. Your ideal recommender has experience in her field (teaching graduate classes is a plus), is passionate about what she teaches, and writes well.

- **Work way, way, *way* in advance.** Professors are busy. Know your deadlines and set up a meeting at least a month before the recommendation is due. Don't pop the question right after class, either: e-mail your professor (see "Sample E-mails," page 47), stop by during office hours, or ask in person for a meeting—then show up on time and make your pitch.

- **Share your story.** Ask politely, but directly, if your professor would be able to write you a strong recommendation letter. But don't stop there. Make this a conversation about what you're passionate about: the coursework you've completed; the school, job, or program you're pursuing; what you've learned in class and how you hope to apply it. These things can inform the letter and also help your recommender learn what you're about.

- **Don't be discouraged if your professor says no.** It doesn't mean he hates you or thinks you'd be better off digging ditches and using your degree as a placemat. He may be writing a book, or buried in research, or serving on committees, or unsure if he knows you well enough to give you the glowing recommendation you deserve. Say thank you, pick out a new professor, and then try again.

- **Come prepared.** Provide your CV or résumé (see page 126), a transcript, and any relevant statements of purpose, writing samples, or previous letters of recommendation. Encourage your professor to ask questions about your experience or skills, and be sure to let her know if there's anything in particular you would like to see highlighted in your letter. Bring any official forms or cover sheets for your professor to submit with the letter, and make all deadlines, length requirements, etc., clear (highlighting and post-it flags are not too much flair).

- **Keep track of your deadlines.** Follow up (gently) by e-mail or in person one week before your materials are due. If your professor drops the ball, don't panic, and definitely don't panic *at him*. You and your academic advisor should be able to hash out a last-minute emergency rescue plan.

- **Recognize that, ultimately, you're asking for a favor.** Say thank you in person, send a note (handwritten, please), and when your dream school/program/employer is appropriately blown away by your stellar accomplishments, tell your prof (and thank her again).

- **Do it yourself.** Sometimes, your teacher will be so bogged down with professorial pursuits that she'll ask you to draft a recommendation to get the ball rolling. More than likely, she will edit and add to it before sending it out, so don't sweat it (and don't forget to use the third person). Start off with an intro sentence (see example, next page), drop in a few specific mentions of your coursework that strengthen your candidacy, and then wrap it up.

Sample Recommendation

To Whom It May Concern:

It is my pleasure to recommend Cecilia for admission to your graduate program. I have known Cecilia for three years and have been consistently impressed with both her strong coursework in my Urban Sustainability seminar and her quick, reliable, and professional work as a teaching assistant for the Environmental Studies department. In a competitive class of over 60 students, Cecilia's grades were routinely at the top, and her term paper on the ecology of city parks deservedly won our annual prize for excellence in independent research. She is a devoted, hardworking, and enthusiastic learner, and I am confident she will be a strong asset to your program.

Sincerely,
Alice Goulet
Professor of Environmental Studies

SOCIAL LIFE

How to Find and Make Friends

The great thing about your college social life is that you're starting fresh. No one knows you from high school or remembers the time you fainted during a chorus concert or lit your beakers on fire in Chemistry. The flip side? No one knows you at all—yet. Finding a brand-new set of friends might feel daunting, but all you have to do is look around: everyone's in this together. Friendship is magic; here are a few tricks.

- **Don't stress!** The first few weeks of college are hugely busy—you have dorms to decorate, classes to pick, parties to attend, and campuses to get lost in. Feeling overwhelmed is normal, so roll with it.

- **Be yourself. Or whoever you want.** College is a lot like the Internet: here, you can be anybody. Don't feel bound by your high-school identity; not only are you now a total stranger to a bunch of other total strangers, you're also less likely to be pigeonholed in

general. College identities are more fluid—
there's no "in" crowd, and no one cares if
you were (or weren't) elected to homecom-
ing court. Don't try to be someone you're
not, but go ahead and be the person you
couldn't be till now.

- **Connect online.** Many schools will organize
online forums or Facebook groups for students to meet one another before arriving
on campus. Check them out, post a comment or two, and get in touch with anyone
who seems interesting, but don't go on a
huge friending spree. Having 300 new con-
tacts isn't much better than having none, it
just takes the sea-of-faces effect online.

- **Show up.** During orientation, your residen-
tial staff will probably throw a host of get-to-
know you events, either mandatory or with
attractive bribes of food. Take advantage—
you'll never have so many potential friends
(or free food) in a single place again. Don't
just grab a snack and peace out (there's a
reason they call them ice cream *socials*); talk
to people, even if it's only to comment on
how camp-counselor-goofy your RA is.

- **Sit down.** The dining hall is a great place to start meeting people: everyone has to eat. Plunk your tray down next to someone who's sitting alone (or in a small group) and strike up a conversation. Suggested topic: how bad the food is. Almost no one will disagree, even if it's pretty good.

- **Keep your door open.** Not just metaphorically. Jam a doorstop in place while you're chilling in your dorm room, and you're more likely to have people pop in. Shutting people out (again, literally) won't help you meet anyone.

- **Hang out outside your room.** Go watch the communal TV instead of cloistering yourself with Netflix. Do your reading in the dorm lounge instead of on your bed. Bring a hacky sack to the quad and party like it's 1999.

- **Share.** You didn't bring that Playstation 3 all the way from home just to play endless solo rounds of Halo, after all. Buy family-sized bags of Doritos and make friends between mouthfuls of MSG. Show off your favorite obscure movies with an impromptu viewing session in your dorm room. Lend out your spare laundry basket.

- **Say yes.** During orientation and the first week or two of classes, your dormmates will likely band together and travel in packs to investigate campus offerings. Walking to advisor appointments? Yes. Getting ID pictures taken? Yes. Milkshake run at 2 a.m.? Absolutely. You can always cull your schedule later, but if you stay solo now, you might miss your window of opportunity.

- **Go to clubs.** Whether it's intramural Ultimate Frisbee or live action role playing in full medieval armor, chances are if you think something's interesting, so does an organized group of your fellow students. If your school offers an activities fair, hit it up and sample the extracurricular buffet. You can also look into cultural, religious, and political activist groups, if that's your thing.

- **Break up your circle.** Being in college with your crew from high school isn't a friendship fait accompli—sticking in your circle will probably keep you from meeting new people, and if your old friends drift apart (hey, it happens), you'll end up with no one to hang with. Branch out.

- **Don't get *too* attached.** It's normal for the friends you make in the first few weeks of college to drift away once all of you get more settled in different social groups. That said, some people do meet their new BFF (or BF/GF) on day one. Just don't cling if you find you and your first friends becoming mere acquaintances.

Six Non-Stupid Conversation Starters

- **Where's everyone from?** Basic, sure, but everyone's gotta come from somewhere, and people do tend to like talking about themselves. If no one answers right off the bat, dive in first and offer up your origin story.

- **That's a cool necklace/hat/tattoo.** Nobody doesn't like compliments, especially about something that's clearly an important part of their appearance. Follow it up with a question:

Where's it from? Handmade? Family heirloom? Result of a crazy misunderstanding at the tattoo parlor?

- **Did anyone else wait for hours to get an ID?** Asking a question about campus life is a good start, since it's something everyone has in common. A little commiseration goes a long way toward building camaraderie.

- **This food totally sucks.** It may not seem particularly charming, but complaining is a quick-'n'-easy way to bond. Besides, everyone has to eat, and barely anyone likes cafeteria food.

- **Anything cool going on tonight?** Especially your first week or two on campus, there's bound to be tons of parties, mixers, shindigs, and other social gatherings sponsored by clubs, departments, sports teams, etc. Use your dormmates as a sounding board to hash out options.

- **Hey.** Sounds too simple, but don't overthink it! Waiting for others to open up and start chatting could get you stuck in a game of Silence Chicken. Speak up and say hi so people know they can approach you.

How to Rush, Pledge, and Go Greek

For students who join the Greek system, being a member of a sorority or fraternity is the ultimate extracurricular. It's enriching and exhilarating (and perhaps résumé-boosting), and in many cases you get to *live* with your friends. Every campus is different, but generally, rush is the period (usually in fall or spring) when the different houses hold events, interviews, dinners, and parties, and then offer bids—invitations to join—to potential candidates (that would be you). Here's how to navigate.

- **Never say never.** Just because you've never pictured yourself in a sorority or fraternity doesn't mean you aren't worthy. If you're curious, investigate during rush and see if the personality of any house appeals to you. Also look into coed fraternities, or service fraternities, which are dedicated to performing community service.

- **Be genuine.** Don't fake a persona just to get in good with your potential brothers or sisters. If you do ultimately join, you'll be stuck with people who don't know the real you, and that's no good.

- **Meet the people.** It's easy to be distracted by the fun and flashy stuff that goes on during rush. Barbecues! Boat cruises! Free breakfast! But rush doesn't last forever. When the dust settles and your membership solidifies, you want to be with brothers/sisters you relate to and like, not just some people who gave you some stuff once. Ask your hosts how they spend a typical weekend, what the living situation is like, and what everyone does outside the house (for starters).

- **Don't be discouraged.** If you don't get the bids that you wanted, don't take it too hard. Rush is an inherently crazy time that makes it nearly impossible to *truly* get to know someone. It's not you, it's them. If you still want to go Greek, try again next round, and find some other cool clubs to keep you occupied in the meantime.

- **Know what you're getting into.** If you get a bid, investigate exactly what membership entails before you sign up. Is the house nationally affiliated and officially recognized by the school? Has it ever been on probation? Is there a campus advisor for Greek life? What are the dues? How much time will you have to put in as a pledge before you become a full-fledged member?

- **It's okay to de-pledge.** Getting swept up in the fun of rush is one thing, but making the commitment is another, and sometimes—for whatever reason—the fit just isn't right. Don't be afraid to withdraw your pledge if you're unsure. It happens, and it's better for everyone than being stuck in a house you aren't 100 percent happy with.

- **It's *not* okay to haze.** Embarrassing, exhausting, or otherwise cruel and unusual initiation rituals aren't business as usual: they're criminal. Any kind of hazing is not only against campus regulations but against the law. Humiliation, binge drinking, and bodily harm in the name of membership is *never* worth it. If your house pressures you to do anything dangerous, don't be a bystander; report it to your Greek advisor, or call 1-888-NOT-HAZE.

How to Get a Date, Reject Someone, or Break Up

When it comes to dating in college, there are plenty of fish in the sea, but you're a little minnow in a big pond. Maybe you have a few high school relationships under your belt, or maybe you're boldly going where you've never gone before. Either way, don't feel any pressure. Above all, college dating is about hanging out and forming friendships that lead to something more—no big deal.

How to Ask Someone Out

1. **Talk first.** Many great college relationships start as friendships. Get to know the object of your affection and establish a little rapport. Sometimes talking about favorite things will give you a direct in ("You've never seen *Twin Peaks*? You have to come over for a marathon.").

2. **Make sure there's interest.** Is the person in question single? Interested in dating? Interested in dating *you*? Hint: anyone who begins phrases with "oh, my boyfriend/girlfriend . . ." is probably not in the market.

3. **Plan something.** Your "date" doesn't have to involve white tablecloths and candlelight. It can be something as basic as a cup of coffee together or a *Dr. Who* marathon in your dorm room. Just have something specific in mind when you ask ("You wanna hang out sometime?" won't cut it).

4. **Make your move.** Asking in person is best, but let's be real: this is college. Pinging someone with an IM or sending a text message is acceptable, especially if you've got something dead simple (read: inexpensive) in mind. Just be prepared for the consequences: it's much easier to reject someone digitally.

5. **Be clear.** Nothing will crush your romantic aspirations faster than the dread "Sounds great, who else is coming?" Try using a direct "you and I" instead of a vague "we" when asking, or mention how much you'd like to hang out "one on one" and get to know each other.

How to Reject Someone

1. **Actually say no . . .** Avoid mixed signals from the get-go. Don't agree to going out simply to spare the person's feelings; you'll just make things worse (for both of you) in the long run.

2. **. . . but be polite.** A gracious "Thanks, I'm flattered, but . . ." will preserve your dignity and theirs.

3. **Be friendly.** If you want to be friends instead of dating, you can certainly say so, but don't give false hope that a romance is possible. And be honest—don't say you're "not looking to date right now" if you're only going to turn around and hook up with someone else the next weekend.

4. **Keep your cool.** If this person is being persistent or won't leave you alone (at a party, say), be polite but firm. Repeat "No, thanks" until they get the message, and seek refuge with a group of your friends if you need to.

How to Break Up with Someone

1. **Be confident.** Before you say anything, do a little soul-searching to make sure the relationship isn't working for you, and stick to your instincts. Be prepared for the other person to disagree, but don't let them talk you out of it.

2. **Be on point.** Think of one or two specific reasons for breaking up. Knowing exactly why you two aren't a good match will help you organize your thoughts. Don't try to tear the other person down.

3. **Consider the timing.** Don't wait until finals week or the night before spring break. Try to pick a time that's relatively low-stress.

4. **Do it in person.** Unlike asking someone out, a breakup requires face-to-face contact. For obvious reasons, avoid public spaces. If you're doing it in your dorm room, ask your roommate to study in the library while you drop the bad news.

5. **Make your case.** Explain your points in a straightforward manner, being firm but polite.

Be prepared to deal with an emotional reaction, but try to keep from getting upset yourself.

6. **Avoid making promises.** Don't say "I want to be friends" if you really don't, and don't send someone packing with false hope that you might get back together. Reassure, and then say goodbye.

7. **You will survive.** If you're the dumpee, don't take it too hard. College is a great time to be single—never again will you surrounded by such a high concentration of potential love interests.

How to Deal with a Long-Distance Relationship

Ah, to be young and in love and about to head off to colleges miles—or states—apart. Deciding to embark on a long-distance relationship (or not) can be heart wrenching, and keeping the romance going isn't much easier. Here's how to handle it.

- **Be sure that this is what you both want.** A long-distance relationship is only as strong as your mutual commitment. If you and your high-school sweetheart truly, madly, deeply believe you have something worth holding onto, then try to hack it out. But if you have doubts, it's better to cut ties sooner rather than later.

- **Have a communication strategy.** Are you two going to Skype? Text? E-mail? Will you need to talk once a day, or will once-a-week catch-ups suffice? Figure out a system, but make sure it's flexible. Your schedules are liable to change in your first semester (or two), and your relationship needs to be able to adapt. If most of your conversations devolve into "What did *you* have for lunch?," you may need to reevaluate the relationship.

- **Get a life.** For the first few weeks of college, you'll both be busy: meeting people, auditing classes, accidentally locking yourself out of your dorm room, and making friends. Don't shortchange yourself by skipping in-person bonding on campus just to get back to your room and videochat with your far-flung significant other. Set up mandatory radio silence between you until you're both settled in.

- **Don't be a martyr.** Suffering in the absence of someone you love doesn't mean you love them more; it just means you're suffering. And suffering sucks. Focus on making friends and engaging with your new environment—you'll have better stories to share with your S.O.

- **Visit wisely.** There are four major factors involved in figuring out a visitation schedule: physical distance, financial/logistical feasibility, how much time you can bear to spend apart, and how many weekends/school breaks you can spare without feeling like you've deserted your college friends. Consider all of these. Unless one of you has a private jet, farther-apart couples will need to resign themselves to once or twice a semester. Closer doesn't necessarily mean easier, though: the stress of commuting back and forth between campuses can frazzle one (or both) of you, so don't expect to sustain an every-weekend schedule.

- **Avoid the resentment trap.** The hardest part about being in a long-distance relationship is the frustrating inability to talk in person when you need to. This can lead to one partner feeling abandoned or ignored, and the other feeling overwhelmed when a conversation finally does take place. The best way to combat this is not to let things fester: if something's bugging you, speak up. Even if you don't have time for a full-blown discussion, let your other half know something's on your mind with a quick "we need to talk" text. Followed by a reassuring "and it's not because I'm going to dump you!" text. Unless . . .

- **When in doubt, break up.** This is hard advice to take, but sometimes the strain is too much. If you're more stressed than psyched about being in a relationship, do the honorable thing and give it a swift, merciful end. It's best to do the deed in person, but this isn't always feasible (or considerate; no one likes traveling hundreds of miles just to get dumped). A phone call or a visit home during a school vacation is your best bet when distance is a major factor. Breaking up is never easy, but college is all about change, and sometimes that means changing without the person you knew and loved in high school. You may need to avoid each other for a while—Thanksgiving-break hookups are tempting, but ultimately they just create more heartache.

How to Entertain Yourself for Cheap

Your time at school is about learning, sure, but you should also—to paraphrase that classic pseudomotivational phraselet—work hard, play hard, and not spend hard. Which is not so hard if you follow this advice.

- **Stay on campus.** College clubs, sports teams, and social groups exist to entertain you, but your options aren't just limited to the Big Game and frat parties. Seek out smaller, more intimate gatherings at everything from swing-dance lessons to tabletop game tournaments to film clubs and cultural societies. Bonus: many clubs offer free food as enticement.

- **Be an urban explorer.** If you're in a big-city school, your freebie options are only as limited as your transit budget. Hit up art galleries, book readings, big events (holiday parades, outdoor markets, etc.), coffeehouse performances, and free outdoor movies and concerts (weather permitting). Heck, even walking around can be awesome if you're in a weird or interesting neighborhood.

- **Make your own fun.** Gather friends and throw shoestring social events like an All-Ramen Dinner Party (BYO toppings), a Bad Film Festival (BYO B movie), a Cheapo Nail Salon Night (BYO polish), or a Really Short Road Trip (BYO gas money).

- **Use the library.** Most universities keep a healthy collection of music, films, even comic books (ahem, *graphic novels*) along with their highfalutin academic tomes.

- **Share.** Share joint custody of a magazine sub-scription with a friend or two, split the cost of a video-streaming service with your roommate, and carpool everywhere.

The Only Spring Break Packing List You'll Ever Need

- T-shirts/tank tops
- Shorts/skirts
- Dresses (if applicable)
- Pajamas/loungewear
- Sneakers
- Sandals/flip-flops
- Nice (nonsandal) shoes
- 1 or 2 dressy outfits for nights
- Underwear
- Towel
- Sunblock
- Chapstick
- Toiletries

- Medication
  (pack it in your carry-on if you're flying)

- Sunglasses

- Two bathing suits
  (so you never have to put on a damp one)

- Beach cover-ups

- Tote bag/backpack

- Water bottle

- Light jacket

- Chargers for your cell phone, e-reader, etc.

- Printouts of your hotel/hostel location
  (in case your phone dies)

How to Deal with Stress and Homesickness

A lot of people who remember college as "the best years of their life" forget just how confusing, stressful, and downright scary those four years can sometimes be. It's not all intellectually stimulating discussions and awesome parties, and feeling overwhelmed and anxious from time to time is totally normal. But if you or one of your friends feels hopeless, stressed out, or persistently withdrawn, more help may be needed. Here's what you need to know.

- **Never feel alone.** More than 75 percent of college students say they feel overwhelmed by their life at school, and over half report feeling "frequently" homesick. Keep that in mind when it seems like everyone but you is a ray of sunshine.

- **Ride it out.** The first few weeks of school can be the hardest. Boarding with complete strangers and facing a host of logistical and social challenges can make you want to dive headfirst back into your high-school bedroom. This feeling is totally normal, and it will fade with time. Work on making friends, even if you have to force yourself (see page 74), throw yourself into classes and clubs you're psyched about, and wait for the feeling to pass.

- **Get some touches of home.** Call home for a quick chat, hang pictures of your hometown friends, or drop major hints about needing a care package. If you're not far from home, a visit *might* be helpful—or make you feel worse. So give yourself enough time to get settled (at least through a week or two of classes) before you hightail it back to the homestead.

- **Know the signs.** Depression and anxiety can manifest in a number of ways, not all of which are obvious and some of which are completely contradictory. Symptoms can include low energy, changes in sleep pattern (insomnia, poor sleep, and/or oversleeping), changes in appetite, decreased ability to focus, thoughts of hopelessness, lack of motivation and/or energy, and physical aches and pains.

- **Make small fixes.** Little glitches in your environment can have a huge impact on mental health. A steady diet of soft-serve and chicken fingers can leave you feeling sluggish and unmotivated (see page 29 for healthy eating options). Exercise (even walking) has been shown to alleviate stress, particularly when done outside or in well-lit gyms. Low levels of sunlight can leave you feeling crabby; invest in a full-spectrum sun lamp, or talk to your doctor about vitamin D supplements.

- **Talk it out.** If you're worried about a friend's mental state, don't bombard him with questions—a frantic "are you depressed?!" can sound more like accusation than inquiry. Instead, ask if anything's bothering him, and then share some of your own worries to spark a conversation. And listen, of course.

- **Seek out the pros.** Today's college campus is incredibly well equipped to help students struggling with emotional issues. Don't ever feel like a problem isn't serious or big enough—the counselors are there to help everyone. It's their job (paid for by your stuition, no less), and you absolutely have a right to seek their support. If going in person is too much to handle, call for an appointment, or e-mail your advisor and ask how to get in touch with a counselor. Whatever your situation, help is there.

- **Important: if you or any of your friends experience or share thoughts of suicide or self-harm, do not wait to get help.** Immediately contact someone with the expertise to help you: an RA, an advisor, a school counselor, or a medical center staff member. If you cannot get in touch with someone on campus, call 1-800-SUICIDE for 24/7 help.

MONEY AND THE REAL WORLD

How to Make Money

You don't need to be an Econ major to know that putting a little cash aside is important (but if you are one, hey, look: maximization, kind of!) Here are some dead simple ways to mix some earning with your learning.

- **Be realistic.** Your job, first and foremost, is to do well in class. No second job should compromise that. Even a part-time gig is a big commitment, so keep your potential work hours realistic. Working ten hours a week or less is correlated with a higher GPA, compared to working more hours.

- **Get a job on campus.** A campus job should be your first target: the commute's negligible, and school departments are used to working around student schedules. Get a résumé in shape (see page 126), and scour your college's online bulletin board for an opening that matches your skills. Part-time employment might be anything from juggling administra-

tive office tasks to shelving library books to working as a TA or research assistant.

- **Get a job off campus.** Hit up establishments in your school's neighborhood for student-friendly employment opportunities and become a barista, delivery guy/gal, receptionist, waitstaff person, or hamburger flipper.

- **Tutor.** Post flyers (real or digital) and rent your brain to fellow students stuck on the finer points of French, calculus, or the Krebs cycle. Alternatively, look into working with SAT- and ACT-prep companies. Or strike out solo helping high-school kids with their college essays—after all, you're a seasoned expert. Check other ads (or ask friends) to find the going hourly rate.

- **Freelance.** Got marketable skills? Market 'em. Use your DSLR to take photos for publications, headshots for models, or snaps of kittens for stock-photography websites. Offer your eagle eye for copyediting thesis projects and term papers. Contact the student newspaper or alumni magazine and offer to cover events (these might not pay . . . but you could build a writing portfolio with clips to

help you get paying gigs). Do friends' laundry for ten bucks a load (folding is extra).

- **Sell your body . . . to science.** Hit up your school's science and psychology departments (many have e-mail list hosts) and take advantage of current research studies that need subjects. You can usually bag anywhere from $1 to $15 a pop for opinion surveys, thought experiments, and mini tests. Longer-term studies (on, say, sleep habits) pay a higher premium, but you may be treated more like a guinea pig than like a human.

- **Babysit.** Hang faculty-friendly flyers near graduate-student or professorial hangouts, offering your sitting services to those who need a break from their kiddos to get some work done. Or post a profile on a website like SitterCity to cast a net beyond campus. If you babysat in high school, ask former clients if you can list them as references.

- **Sell your stuff.** Get rid of old textbooks (see page 106). Hunt down a consignment shop and sell clothes you don't want. Auction off your old computer on eBay. Create an Etsy store for your hand-knit scarves. Pawn your

old furniture to your friends (or the next crop of incoming freshmen).

- **Take notes.** If your school offers notetaking services for students with disabilities, you might earn money by taking transcriptions in lectures. Check with your student services department to find out where your stenographic skills are needed.

- **Team up.** For work that requires many hands, grab some friends and hire yourselves out as a band of roving jacks (or janes) of all trades. Yardwork, moving, painting, cleaning, or dog walking are all good group options.

How to Avoid Going Broke on Textbooks

Textbooks are pricey, but there are ways to avoid forking over hefty premiums to the college bookstore. Try these alternatives when a new semester rolls around.

- **Don't buy new, and don't buy from the bookstore.** Yes, the campus bookstore is convenient. But you're almost guaranteed to get the worst deal there. If you have no other alternative, see if your school's brick-and-mortar establishment offers used copies or a buy-back policy.

- **Get the number.** To make book hunting a snap, use your smartphone to take quick pics of ISBNs (the string of numbers above the barcode or on the copyright page) at the bookstore.

- **Buy online.** Plug the book's ISBN into used-book sites like AbeBooks and Half.com, or search eBay for secondhand copies. If your school has online classifieds, search those or post a request.

- **Find hand-me-downs.** Even if you're taking Accelerated Introduction to Old Icelandic, chances are someone on campus has taken the course before. Seek out older students in your major and see if you (and a few Presidents Jackson) can't convince them to part with their old copies. Also be alert for used-textbook sales sponsored by campus groups and clubs, usually held at the beginning of a semester.

- **Go international.** Some publishers create "international editions" of their books (with different covers and ISBNs, but identical contents) to be sold outside U.S. markets at a much lower price. A little Google-fu can usually track these down. If you're looking for hard-to-find foreign-language literature, hit up online bookstores based abroad: even with international shipping, it can sometimes be cheaper to order them.

- **Rent.** For a slightly lower premium, you can borrow a textbook from a rental company on a semester- or year-long basis. Again, don't rely on your campus bookstore for the best deal—search the Internet first.

- **Share.** If you're going to form a study group (see page 49) or have a few friends in the same class, go halvsies (or quartersies) on a book—just make sure you have a rock-solid joint custody plan.

- **Use the library copy.** Check the syllabus and assignment list. Does your instructor require long readings from the textbook for every class, or will you dip into it only occasionally? Library textbooks are likely to be on limited loan periods (think hours, not days), but if it seems feasible to hole up with the book once a week, you can save money.

- **Sell back.** Reverse the process: most used-book websites are also sellers' marketplaces, your fellow students are likely to need a copy, and sometimes even the campus bookstore will take sloppy seconds. Trust us, in three years, you won't care about owning *Principles*

of Microeconomics, unless you need a really good doorstop. Sell sooner rather than later, while your edition is still current; planned obsolescence moves fast even in dead-tree media.

- **Opt for an old edition.** For works of literature and other books that don't contain edition-sensitive materials (e.g., problem sets that will need to match what your prof assigns), look for bargains on vintage editions. Used bookstores will often have multiple copies of classic works for pennies a copy. If the text in question is a translation or other adaptation, double-check you've got the right one; not all *Odysseys* are created equal.

How to Ask Your Parents for Money

Your parents have already given you so much—
life, love, a roof over your head, maybe even this
book. But sometimes you need a little extra to tide
you over. Cash, that is. Here's how to plead your
case.

- **Do it in person.** Ask when you're home for
  a visit, or over the phone if you're in a pinch.
  Letters are acceptable if you have patience
  (and stationery), but e-mail (or, God forbid,
  texting) should be an emergency last resort.

- **Single out one parent.** Having a one-to-one
  conversation puts the odds more in your favor.

- **Be positive.** Talk about your life at school
  and ask about theirs before grabbing for the
  checkbook. Soften the ground by dropping a
  few hints about your accomplishments and how
  hard you've been working (but don't overdo it).

- **Be specific,** amount-wise and purpose-wise. Ask for an exact amount of money to put toward a concrete need: $150 for textbooks, $50 for groceries, $25 for dues in the "Double-Secret Exclusive Pre-Med/Pre-Law/Pre-Business Honor Students Association." If the money's for a service—fixing your computer, say, or an application fee for study abroad—emphasize all the intangible things the money will help you do.

- **Leave room to maneuver.** It never hurts to aim a little higher than necessary; that way, your parents can feel like they bargained you down while you still get the money you need. Be willing to negotiate, take less than you need, or accept the money as a "loan" (unless they insist on oppressive interest rates).

- **Be mature.** Don't whine, beg, or bad-mouth them if they say no. Act like an adult and they'll treat you like one.

- **Say thank you.** Once right after they say yes, and again later, once you've bought whatever you need.

How to Get Discounts on Everything

Full price? Please. That's for people with income. Smart college students pay pennies on the dollar for . . . well, everything. That poorly photographed student ID of yours is, in fact, a golden ticket. Some examples:

- Any venue where student attendance is desired will probably cut you a deal: museums, theaters, clubs, movies, sporting events, conventions, concerts, gyms, etc.

- Sign up for as many rewards programs as your e-mail inbox can stand. If you have a smartphone, search for "loyalty card" apps to keep digital copies (and keep your wallet from bloating).

- If you're at the mall, many clothing stores (think J. Crew and Ann Taylor) and fast-food joints (from Arby's to Qdoba) have student discounts—they just don't mention them. It

never hurts to ask at the register, even if there's no signage.

- Computer hardware and software usually come at some generic discount to students, but check with your school's IT department and see if they don't have even sweeter deals for you.

- If your school has an agreement with a cell phone carrier, Internet service provider, bank, or credit card company, check it out, but don't go in blindly. Comparison shop, read the fine print, and don't get yourself caught in a nasty contract.

- Transit authorities typically offer lower-cost passes to students, especially if you're in an area with a scholar-heavy populace. Train, coach bus, and occasionally even airline tickets can be had for less, too; search the Internet for "student travel fares."

- Some insurance companies will knock a few bucks off your car insurance premium if you get good grades; check with them (or your parents, if they're the ones footing the bill).

- If you write for a campus publication, your editors might be able to hook you up with "comp"

(read: free) tickets to local plays, concerts, or cultural events (provided you write something about them, of course).

- Subscribe to the local branch of a deal-a-day website like Groupon, Google Offers, or LivingSocial (or visit sites that aggregate all the offers in your area so you don't get spammed to death).

- Newspapers and magazines occasionally offer bargain subscriptions for students—or you can peruse them for free at your school's library.

- When it doubt, ask. Even if there isn't an official policy for students, a winning smile and youthful disposition can go a long way to bagging an under-the-table discount. Most businesses would rather have you pay a discount on something than buy nothing at all (and you can reward their kindness by becoming a loyal customer).

How to Be Smart with a Credit Card

Having fun isn't hard when you've got a credit card! But that's kind of the problem: it's *really* easy to get yourself into debt when you're a student. And while lots of college-age mistakes will fade with time, consumer debt does the opposite. Not only will your interest rate add to your tab as the years go on, your credit score could take a serious hit, making it hard to get approved for student loans, car financing, and mortgages. So play your cards right:

- **You don't need a credit card.** The card *can* be a powerful tool to build a credit history if you use it wisely, but it's not free money. You can get along fine without one: a debit card from your bank will take care of almost any transaction that needs credit card numbers (online purchases, say). And don't be tempted by swag: free sunglasses are indeed

awesome, but a staggering APR is not, and many cards aren't easily terminated (despite the promise of CANCEL AT ANY TIME).

- **Pick a winner.** An ideal card has a low APR (annual percentage rate, or how much it will cost you to "borrow" money with your credit card) and no annual fee. Rewards programs can be great, but don't sign up to get cash back if you have to pay a fee for the privilege. Websites like NerdWallet can customize a comparison of credit cards based on how much you plan to spend.

- **Read the fine print.** Make sure you know how your card's default interest rate works (it's the rate you will pay as penalty for making a late payment or pay less than the minimum). Look at the change of terms policy and understand that your card issuer can raise your rates even if you pay on time (yes, it's totally unfair!). Under the practice known as universal default, your credit issuer reserves the right to jack up your interest rate if you fall behind on bills with other creditors, so keeping your credit history as spotless as possible is important.

- **Pay on time.** Know when your statement comes in and when your payment is due. If you have an online checking account, see if you can schedule an automatic monthly payment of the minimum required by the card, and then follow up with the balance when you have time.

- **Don't spend on stuff you can't afford.** If you can't pay cash for something, think carefully before charging it. Never use a card to finance your living expenses or your education. Emergencies are fine (a cab ride home, for example), but don't lie to yourself about the direness of a situation to justify swiping plastic.

- **Know your limits.** Your credit limit is the maximum amount you're permitted to charge. A sky-high limit is exciting (and flattering) but hard to resist. But do be realistic: if your limit is too low and you charge almost up to the line (like $700 out of $1,000), your credit score (see below) could go down. High credit scores are correlated with people who use about 10 percent of available credit, so crunch some numbers for your situation and extrapolate.

- **Keep score.** Your credit score is a number that represents how worthy you are of credit, based on your spending history. The better your record (paying bills on time, not exceeding your credit limit), the higher your score. Banks use it, but so do mobile phone companies, landlords, insurance companies, and government departments. You don't need to obsess over the exact statistics, but you should have an idea of what it is and what things affect it. Opening up a bunch of new credit cards (including store-brand cards), leaving utility bills unpaid, and even asking to look up your credit report can lower your score. Under the Fair and Accurate Credit Transactions Act, U.S. residents are entitled to one free credit report from each of the three major credit reporting agencies every 12 months, so a check-in once a year is a good idea.

- **Don't subscribe.** Whether you're signing up for World of Warcraft or *Cosmopolitan*, be wary of automatic payment plans—these are an easy way to incur charges on your card without realizing it.

- **Avoid cash advances.** Getting cash via your credit card is always a bad deal. The interest rate on a cash advance is usually higher than the rate for purchases made with the card. And your issuer will apply your payments to the lower-interest items first, meaning you'll carry the debt with the highest interest (i.e., cash advances) the longest.

- **Let there be only one.** One credit card is all you need to start, and opening multiple cards can hurt your credit score even if you pay the statements on time.

How to Interview a Landlord

There's a reason you don't often see college apartments featured in glossy lifestyle magazines: they're not exactly known for their shiny (or functional, for that matter) amenities. Signing a lease for your own place is exciting (even if your parents are technically the ones signing), but don't move too fast—that scribbled signature on the dotted line can stick you with some pretty awful digs. If you're planning a move off campus and it's your first time being lord or lady of your own nondorm domain, here's a crash course in apartment inspection.

Entrance

- Does the apartment door have a deadbolt? What about the front door of the building? Is there a buzzer?

- How and where do you receive mail? Is there a safe place for packages to be delivered?

- Is there a secure area for bike storage?

- Who is responsible for clearing/salting the walkway if it snows?

Interior

- Check the size of doorways and rooms; make sure you can actually fit your furniture through and in them.

- Which way do the windows face (i.e., will you get any light)? Are there even windows to begin with? If there is a fire escape near a window (or if you're on the ground floor), does that window lock securely?

- Examine the ceilings and walls—are there remnants of leaks (water stains, peeling paint or tile)? Is everything clean? Do you have enough outlets in convenient locations (with three prongs, if needed)?

- Is there a washer and dryer in the building (or, if you're living the luxuriant life, in your apartment)?

Do they work? How much do they cost to use? If you'll need a laundromat, is there one nearby?

- Count and measure the closets—is there enough space for your clothes, shoes, and other stuff? What about built-in bookshelves and cabinets?

Kitchen

- Is the oven gas/electric/ceramic (and will this affect your utility bills)? Test it; make sure it turns on and off safely.

- Check under the sinks; look for damage or leaks (or, God forbid, cockroaches).

- Open the fridge and inspect the interior (you might look crazy, but not as crazy as you'll feel if you find something nasty in there later).

- Are there smoke alarms and carbon monoxide detectors? In most areas these are required by law, but you'll really want them in any case.

- If you're lucky enough to have a dishwasher, look inside and check for potential damage (drips, bad seal around the edge, chipped countertop above it).

- Make sure there's enough space to store and prepare food (even if all you need is a square foot of Formica for your George Foreman grill.

Bathroom

- Look under the sink and in and around the tub/shower and toilet for signs of bad plumbing (cracks, leaks) or bugs.

- Flush the toilet and turn on taps and showers. Remember, you'll be left high and dry if they don't work well.

Neighborhood

- Are you reasonably close to campus or some acceptable method of transportation?

- How far are you from bus or train stops? The grocery store? A decent pizza place (or one that delivers quickly)?

- Is the area safe? Check your school's online police log (if available) or search online for "local crime reports" with the apartment's address.

Questions for Your Landlord

- Where does the landlord live? How long has he had the building? How do you get in touch with him if there is an issue?

- Have there been any pest problems?

- Are maintenance and extermination fees covered? Is there a dedicated maintenance staff or just some dude slapping duct tape on everything? (Compare this to what is stated in your lease.)

- Why are the current tenants moving? Can you speak with them about the apartment? (If there's something wrong with the place, you want to know now rather than later.)

- What utilities are covered in the rent payment? Hot water? Normal water? Trash and sewer?

- Does each apartment have its own boiler, or do all tenants share hot water?

- Does the apartment come with A/C? If not, is it capable of handling A/C units?

- Can you control your own heating/cooling (i.e., is there a thermostat)?

- Are you allowed to hang pictures and curtains and drill into the walls? Can you paint?

- When is rent due? Is there a grace period? How is rent collected? Can your parents cosign your lease? Will you need to pay a security deposit and/or an extra month's rent up front?

- Is subletting possible if you go away for a semester/summer?

- Is the apartment cable-ready? If so, what is the service provider? If not, how fast can you get an Internet connection?

- Is the building smoke free and pet free? Do any children live there? Are there quiet hours?

- Will the apartment be cleaned/painted before you move in?

- When will you be allowed to move in?

How to Write a Killer Résumé

You know what they say about résumés and opinions (and some other things): everyone's got one. Furthermore, everyone's got an opinion *about* résumés—always list an objective, never list an objective, no bullet points, yes bullet points, 12-point Times New Roman or may the employment gods strike you dead . . . But everyone agrees that you need one, whether you're after a part-time position, a summer internship, or a Real Job in the Real World. Here's a starter kit of best practices; for more in-depth analysis (and expert proofreading), visit your campus career center.

- **Structure:** The most basic résumé should have four parts: contact information at the top, education and experience in the middle, and skills, references, and awards, certifications, and relevant hobbies at the bottom.

- **Formatting:** Simple is always best. Use a readable serif font (like Times New Roman, Palatino, or Century). Bold or underline the

section headers, and use basic bullet points. Keep everything aligned by creating a table and set the cell borders to "none." Fit everything onto one sheet of paper, using both sides if needed.

- **Basic information:** Include your name, addresses (your dorm and your home, aka "permanent," address), phone number, and school e-mail address.

- **Education:** List your degree program and major (if you've declared), anticipated graduation year, and the name and location of your school. If you've won any honors, scholarships, or awards, list them here; include your GPA only if it's decent.

- **Experience:** This is the biggest (and most important) part of your résumé. List all the jobs you've held, starting with the most recent and working back to your first. Include your job title, the name and location of the employer, and the dates you worked. Underneath each job, include one to three bullet points that detail your duties, responsibilities, and achievements.

- **Use specific, past-tense verbs** (see "Good Verbs to Use in Your Résumé" on page 130)

when describing your experience, and don't
say "I"; sentence fragments are standard here.
As much as possible, illustrate how your
actions created positive change; instead of
Sold magazine subscriptions, write *Increased
subscriber base by 25 percent* (numbers and
figures are helpful). Highlight any time you
led projects or were otherwise in charge;
leadership is a major plus.

- **When it comes to high school jobs, use
your judgment.** A summer spent pulling
weeds might be better omitted (unless you're
really passionate about lawn care), but three
consecutive years working as a camp counselor
shows a great deal of responsibility.

- **Volunteer gigs:** Generally speaking, a significant volunteer or extracurricular position is fair
game for your experience section, especially if
it's relevant to the job you're after. For example:
if you oversee a monthly blood drive for your
school's Red Cross chapter and want to work in
public health, or if you edit a literary magazine
and are angling for a job in publishing.

- **The last section:** This is a contentious zone.
Some career counselors decry having an

"interests" section, while some employers say it's the first place they look. Ultimately, it comes down to relevance: a bank probably won't care if you're an avid rock climber, but a sporting goods store will. For skills, list all your relevant abilities, being as specific as possible (e.g., *Proficient in Adobe Creative Suites, Macromedia Flash, and Microsoft Excel* rather than *Able to use computers*).

- **References:** List them at the bottom of your résumé if you have space. If not, don't sweat it; a simple "References available upon request" is standard.

- **Print it out:** Proofread a hard copy of your résumé. You're almost guaranteed to catch typos you'll miss onscreen. Read it out loud (seriously) and make sure it sounds like a (competent, experienced) human wrote it. Ask as many people as possible to eyeball it for errors.

- **File format:** If you're submitting your résumé digitally, follow any directions provided by your potential employer. If they don't specify a file type, Microsoft Word (.doc, not the insidious .docx) is a near-universal standard.

Good Verbs to Use in Your Résumé

----- LEADERSHIP AND SUPERVISION -----

analyzed	guided	raised
assessed	influenced	reviewed
assumed responsibility	initiated	strengthened
	led	supervised
conducted	managed	transformed
directed	originated	updated
established		

----- ACTION AND ORGANIZATION -----

administered	developed	retrieved
assembled	distributed	scheduled
built	increased	secured
calculated	logged	sold
coordinated	ordered	tracked
designed	organized	
determined	processed	

——— PLANNING AND PROBLEM-SOLVING ———

anticipated	ensured	revamped
applied	expedited	satisfied
brainstormed	found	solved
conceived	gained	strategized
decided	investigated	studied
diagnosed	repaired	tailored

——— CREATIVITY AND COMMUNICATION ———

adapted	illustrated	summarized
briefed	interviewed	surveyed
composed	proofread	synthesized
critiqued	publicized	taught
drafted	reported	verified
edited	shaped	wrote
highlighted	specified	

Sample Resume

Jane Q. Student
School address: 123 Ivory Tower Way,
Room 45B, Collegetown, PA 19123
Permanent address: 4567 Small Street,
Hometown, PA 19000
555-555-5555 | jqstudent@worthington.edu

EDUCATION
Bachelor of Arts, French Literature, anticipated
  May 2016
Worthington College, Collegetown, PA
Current GPA 3.74

Loreland High School, Hometown, PA
Diploma, 2012

EXPERIENCE
Journalism Intern, June 2013–August 2013
The Daily Dispatch, New York, New York
- Reported on local arts and cultural events for biweekly newspaper; blogged daily for ArtsBeat column
- Proofread and edited various articles in page

proofs; assisted with production and design in
InDesign

- Wrote promotional copy for in-house advertisements

Senior Counselor, June 2012–August 2012
Camp Timbertops, Timbertops, Pennsylvania
- Directed and supervised groups of 6- to 8-year-old campers for two-week overnight sessions

- Led and conducted weekendlong wilderness
backpacking trips; responsible for food, safety,
and direction of campers

Hostess, September 2011–May 2012
Le Bon Fromage, Hometown, Pennsylvania
- Provided prompt service in high-volume,
upscale restaurant while taking orders, serving
food, and closing checks

AWARDS AND ACHIVEMENTS
National Merit Scholar, 2012
- First Place, Study Abroad Essay Competition,
Spring 2013

- Emerging Journalist Award, Fall 2013

How to Ace an Interview

Interviews aren't just for jobs: many scholarships, study abroad programs, and campus leadership positions will want to sit you down and evaluate you in person. But don't panic. Think of interviews as conversations, rather than interrogations, and then go get 'em, tiger!

- **Prepare.** Know what job, position, or program you're applying for, the name of your interviewer (and their position at the company), and brainstorm how you might answer typical interview questions (see "Ten Interview Questions to Have Down Cold," page 138).

- **Dress neatly.** Interview attire differs depending on the job and industry, but looking a slob is always a bad idea. For most jobs, a baseline business-casual outfit is safe: collared long-sleeve shirt and tie for men, or blouse (sleeves at least elbow -length) for women. Dark pants, khakis, or skirt (at least knee length, with pantyhose) and low-heeled, dark

shoes. Keep jewelry and makeup to a minimum, and do not wear perfume—you never know who's allergic. Avoid anything too tight or too dirty or too denim.

- **Be on time.** Well ahead of time, figure out how you're going to get to the interview. Calculate how long it will take you to get there and then add 15 minutes; leave at least that much time to travel. Have your interviewer's contact info on hand in case an emergency springs up and you realize you're going to be late (the sooner you can let them know, the better).

- **Bring handouts.** Take a few copies of your résumé and cover letter to the interview. Although you already submitted these materials when you applied, the interviewer might not bring them along, and you might meet with multiple people while you're there.

- **Be polite and friendly** with any receptionists, security guards, or assistants. Some hirers will check with them to see how you acted outside of their office. Don't arrive eating, drinking, or listening to music. Turn your phone off, too.

- **Greet the interviewer with a good, firm handshake,** a relaxed smile, and a sincere "Hello, nice to meet you."

- **Maintain good posture throughout.** Even if your answers are on point, lazy lolling in your chair makes you look . . . lazy.

- **Have examples of your skills at the ready.** It's good to say you're responsible, and even better to illustrate that fact with a two-sentence story about how you handily took over your manager's duties at the fro-yo stand when she came down with lactose intolerance.

- **Make it a perfect match.** Think about what the company has or does that makes it appealing to you, and then connect that to your skills and experience. Employers want someone who wants to work *there*, not just anywhere.

- **Stumped by a question?** Don't be afraid to pause. Respond with "That's a good question," and give yourself a moment to think. A well-composed answer after a few seconds of silence is much better than two minutes of incoherent, nervous rambling.

- **When it's over, say thank you** (good hand-shake again!). Double-check that you have the interviewer's contact info, and send a thank-you note as soon as possible. An e-mail is okay, but a handwritten note—even if it's short—will make you both memorable and responsible in their eyes.

- **Keep your reactions to yourself.** Whether you feel like you aced every question or more like you're totally sunk, it's tempting to whip out your phone for a little social-media com-miseration. Resist the temptation to throw up an "omg worst/best interview EVER!!" status update; you never know who might see it. You might want to share with a few friends in person, but avoid going into too much detail. When it comes to jobs, professionalism starts before you do.

Ten Interview Questions to Have Down Cold

1. **"Tell me about yourself."** If you're stumped, go chronological: birth, growing up, coming to college. Hit on some of your interests along the way, if you can.

2. **"Why did you choose your major?"** Explain what excites you about your studies; use specific readings, courses, or lab work to back it up. If you major in something quote-unquote useless, don't apologize for it. Just be prepared to explain why this is in fact a practical choice, focusing on tangibles like critical thinking, writing skills, or attention to detail.

3. **"Why do you want this job/scholarship/ graduate program?"** The point of this question is twofold: to make sure you're passionate, and to make sure you're actually paying attention to what the position in question is.

4. **"What strengths will you bring?"** Back up every skill with an example of how you've used it in the past; stories make people remember things.

5. **"What's one of your biggest achievements?"** This doesn't have to be something like curing cancer at the top of Mount Everest—if it's personally significant, and, more important, if you grew from the experience, tell the story.

6. **"What's your biggest weakness?"** Don't give a self-serving answer like "I work too hard, ha ha ha!" Don't reveal your deepest insecurity, either. Be honest, pick something that's reasonable and improvable, and follow your shortcoming with a *but* statement (e.g., "I occasionally lose track of details, but I've made a habit of keeping to-do lists on my phone so I don't forget").

7. **"Where do you see yourself in five years?"** This one's tricky—there's no right answer, but very few wrong ones. Open up and share your dreams, as well as how hard you plan to work to achieve them.

8. **"Tell me about your previous jobs."** Here's another excellent opportunity for story time: tell tales of previous employment with anecdotes that demonstrate how you assumed responsibilities or acted in leadership roles.

9. **"How would you describe your work style?"** Walk your interviewer through a typical day of work or a study session, with as much detail as possible. Always mention how well you work on teams: you're trying to join one, after all.

10. **"How would you handle an irate customer/an unexpected error/a high-pressure decision?"** Always begin by saying you'd think it through—no boss wants to hire a knee-jerk reactionary. Deconstruct the problem as best you can, and proceed in a calm, rational way. Chances are the interviewer isn't expecting a specific solution but wants to hear what you'd do if you were in over your head.

How to Deliver a Commencement Speech

Congratulations! Being the one to send off your classmates with words of wisdom is hugely exciting—so exciting, in fact, that it can make you want to throw up into your mortarboard. But it's also an honor, and if you're up there, you've earned it. So prove 'em right!

- **Consider your audience.** Your fellow students will all be out there, of course, but so will faculty, staff, family members, and anyone who happens to walk by the quad. Make your message one that everyone can understand, and keep inside jokes to a minimum.

- **Give your speech a purpose.** Excepting obviously inappropriate topics, a graduation speech can be about anything—which can make knowing where to start daunting. Instead, think about what you want your speech to do. How do you want your audience to feel? Think

of an anecdote, quote, or memory that inspires that feeling, and then put it on paper.

- **Know where to go.** Graduation week is crazy busy, and it's easy to space out during logistical rehearsals. Pay attention to when and where you need to be, and make sure you know how to get on and off stage—you want people to remember your speech, not your tumble down the stairs afterward.

- **Don't memorize.** Even if you're a seasoned thesp who can spit out Shakespearean monologues by heart, don't take chances. Print out your speech in bigger-than-usual type (size 24 is not too big!), double-space it, and put extra space between paragraphs.

- **Stay sharp.** It's hard not to go out with your friends the night before the big day—you totally deserve it, after all—but you've only got one shot at delivering a memorable speech. Save all your celebrations for after graduation, and get a good night's sleep. Drink water before bed and as soon as you wake up to keep yourself from getting hoarse.

- **Take deep breaths.** If you're feeling day-of butterflies, put a hand on your stomach and inhale slowly for a count of five. Repeat until you feel calm.

- **Speak slowly.** Just because you have a time limit doesn't mean you have to sprint to the finish line. Speak at least twice as slowly as you think you need to—in the heat of the moment, it's hard to gauge how fast you're going. If you stumble or get flustered, just pause, inhale, and keep going—no need to apologize.

- **Say "thank you."** You've come a long way, and a lot of people helped you get there.

Acknowledgments

Thanks to everyone at Quirk Books—you are wonderful and terrific, and I'm so proud of what we do. Thanks to my family for encouraging me to follow my dreams of obscure academic disciplines. Thanks to the University of Chicago for accepting a bad romance novel as an application essay; to the advisors, professors, and resident heads there for helping me not just survive but thrive; and, finally, to all my friends for enriching my college life as my knowledge grew.

Also Available:

Stuff Every Man
Should Know

Stuff Every Woman
Should Know